T0334933

THE JPS B'NAI MITZVAH TORAH COMMENTARY

Shemot (Exodus 1:1–6:1)
Haftarah (Isaiah 27:6–28:13; 29:22–23)

Rabbi Jeffrey K. Salkin

The Jewish Publication Society · Philadelphia
University of Nebraska Press · Lincoln

© 2018 by Rabbi Jeffrey K. Salkin. All rights reserved.
Published by The University of Nebraska Press as a
Jewish Publication Society book.
Manufactured in the United States of America
♾

INTRODUCTION

News flash: the most important thing about becoming bar or bat mitzvah isn't the party. Nor is it the presents. Nor even being able to celebrate with your family and friends—as wonderful as those things are. Nor is it even standing before the congregation and reading the prayers of the liturgy—as important as that is.

No, the most important thing about becoming bar or bat mitzvah is sharing Torah with the congregation. And why is that? Because of all Jewish skills, that is the most important one.

Here is what is true about rites of passage: you can tell what a culture values by the tasks it asks its young people to perform on their way to maturity. In American culture, you become responsible for driving, responsible for voting, and yes, responsible for drinking responsibly.

In some cultures, the rite of passage toward maturity includes some kind of trial, or a test of strength. Sometimes, it is a kind of "outward bound" camping adventure. Among the Maasai tribe in Africa, it is traditional for a young person to hunt and kill a lion. In some Hispanic cultures, fifteen year-old girls celebrate the *quinceañera*, which marks their entrance into maturity.

What is Judaism's way of marking maturity? It combines both of these rites of passage: *responsibility* and *test*. You show that you are on your way to becoming a *responsible* Jewish adult through a public *test* of strength and knowledge—reading or chanting Torah, and then teaching it to the congregation.

This is the most important Jewish ritual mitzvah (commandment), and that is how you demonstrate that you are, truly, bar or bat mitzvah—old enough to be responsible for the mitzvot.

What Is Torah?

So, what exactly is the Torah? You probably know this already, but let's review.

The Torah (teaching) consists of "the five books of Moses," sometimes also called the *chumash* (from the Hebrew word *chameish*, which means "five"), or, sometimes, the Greek word Pentateuch (which means "the five teachings").

Here are the five books of the Torah, with their common names and their Hebrew names.

> **Genesis (The beginning), which in Hebrew is Bere'shit (from the first words—"When God began to create").** Bere'shit spans the years from Creation to Joseph's death in Egypt. Many of the Bible's best stories are in Genesis: the creation story itself; Adam and Eve in the Garden of Eden; Cain and Abel; Noah and the Flood; and the tales of the Patriarchs and Matriarchs, Abraham, Isaac, Jacob, Sarah, Rebekah, Rachel, and Leah. It also includes one of the greatest pieces of world literature, the story of Joseph, which is actually the oldest complete novel in history, comprising more than one-quarter of all Genesis.

> **Exodus (Getting out), which in Hebrew is Shemot (These are the names).** Exodus begins with the story of the Israelite slavery in Egypt. It then moves to the rise of Moses as a leader, and the Israelites' liberation from slavery. After the Israelites leave Egypt, they experience the miracle of the parting of the Sea of Reeds (or "Red Sea"); the giving of the Ten Commandments at Mount Sinai; the idolatry of the Golden Calf; and the design and construction of the Tabernacle and of the ark for the original tablets of the law, which our ancestors carried with them in the desert. Exodus also includes various ethical and civil laws, such as "You shall not wrong a stranger or oppress him, for you were strangers in the land of Egypt" (22:20).

> **Leviticus (about the Levites), or, in Hebrew, Va-yikra' (And God called).** It goes into great detail about the kinds of sacrifices that the ancient Israelites brought as offerings; the laws of ritual purity; the animals that were permitted and forbidden for eating (the beginnings of the tradition of kashrut, the Jewish dietary laws); the diagnosis of various skin diseases; the ethical laws of holiness; the ritual calendar of the Jewish year; and various agricultural laws concerning the treatment of the Land of Israel. Leviticus is basically the manual of ancient Judaism.

> Numbers (because the book begins with the census of the Israelites), or, in Hebrew, Be-midbar (In the wilderness). The book describes the forty years of wandering in the wilderness and the various rebellions against Moses. The constant theme: "Egypt wasn't so bad. Maybe we should go back." The greatest rebellion against Moses was the negative reports of the spies about the Land of Israel, which discouraged the Israelites from wanting to move forward into the land. For that reason, the "wilderness generation" must die off before a new generation can come into maturity and finish the journey.

> Deuteronomy (The repetition of the laws of the Torah), or, in Hebrew, Devarim (The words). The final book of the Torah is, essentially, Moses's farewell address to the Israelites as they prepare to enter the Land of Israel. Here we find various laws that had been previously taught, though sometimes with different wording. Much of Deuteronomy contains laws that will be important to the Israelites as they enter the Land of Israel—laws concerning the establishment of a monarchy and the ethics of warfare. Perhaps the most famous passage from Deuteronomy contains the *Shema*, the declaration of God's unity and uniqueness, and the *Ve-ahavta*, which follows it. Deuteronomy ends with the death of Moses on Mount Nebo as he looks across the Jordan Valley into the land that he will not enter.

Jews read the Torah in sequence—starting with Bere'shit right after Simchat Torah in the autumn, and then finishing Devarim on the following Simchat Torah. Each Torah portion is called a parashah (division; sometimes called a *sidrah*, a place in the order of the Torah reading). The stories go around in a full circle, reminding us that we can always gain more insights and more wisdom from the Torah. This means that if you don't "get" the meaning this year, don't worry—it will come around again.

And What Else? The Haftarah

We read or chant the Torah from the Torah scroll—the most sacred thing that a Jewish community has in its possession. The Torah is written without vowels, and the ability to read it and chant it is part of the challenge and the test.

But there is more to the synagogue reading. Every Torah reading has an accompanying haftarah reading. Haftarah means "conclusion," because there was once a time when the service actually ended with that reading. Some scholars believe that the reading of the haftarah originated at a time when non-Jewish authorities outlawed the reading of the Torah, and the Jews read the haftarah sections instead. In fact, in some synagogues, young people who become bar or bat mitzvah read very little Torah and instead read the entire haftarah portion.

The haftarah portion comes from the Nevi'im, the prophetic books, which are the second part of the Jewish Bible. It is either read or chanted from a Hebrew Bible, or maybe from a booklet or a photocopy.

The ancient sages chose the haftarah passages because their themes reminded them of the words or stories in the Torah text. Sometimes, they chose *haftarah* with special themes in honor of a festival or an upcoming festival.

Not all books in the prophetic section of the Hebrew Bible consist of prophecy. Several are historical. For example:

The book of Joshua tells the story of the conquest and settlement of Israel.

The book of Judges speaks of the period of early tribal rulers who would rise to power, usually for the purpose of uniting the tribes in war against their enemies. Some of these leaders are famous: Deborah, the great prophetess and military leader, and Samson, the biblical strong man.

The books of Samuel start with Samuel, the last judge, and then move to the creation of the Israelite monarchy under Saul and David (approximately 1000 BCE).

The books of Kings tell of the death of King David, the rise of King Solomon, and how the Israelite kingdom split into the Northern Kingdom of Israel and the Southern Kingdom of Judah (approximately 900 BCE).

And then there are the books of the prophets, those spokesmen for God whose words fired the Jewish conscience. Their names are immortal: Isaiah, Jeremiah, Ezekiel, Amos, Hosea, among others.

Someone once said: "There is no evidence of a biblical prophet ever being invited back a second time for dinner." Why? Because the prophets were tough. They had no patience for injustice, apathy, or hypocrisy. No one escaped their criticisms. Here's what they taught:

> ▸ God commands the Jews to behave decently toward one another. In fact, God cares more about basic ethics and decency than about ritual behavior.
> ▸ God chose the Jews *not* for special privileges, but for special duties to humanity.
> ▸ As bad as the Jews sometimes were, there was always the possibility that they would improve their behavior.
> ▸ As bad as things might be now, it will not always be that way. Someday, there will be universal justice and peace. Human history is moving forward toward an ultimate conclusion that some call the Messianic Age: a time of universal peace and prosperity for the Jewish people and for all the people of the world.

Your Mission—To Teach Torah to the Congregation

On the day when you become bar or bat mitzvah, you will be reading, or chanting, Torah—in Hebrew. You will be reading, or chanting, the haftarah—in Hebrew. That is the major skill that publicly marks the becoming of bar or bat mitzvah. But, perhaps even more important than that, you need to be able to teach something about the Torah portion, and perhaps the haftarah as well.

And that is where this book comes in. It will be a very valuable resource for you, and your family, in the b'nai mitzvah process.

Here is what you will find in it:

> ▸ A brief **summary** of every Torah portion. This is a basic overview of the portion; and, while it might not refer to everything in the Torah portion, it will explain its most important aspects.
> ▸ A list of the **major ideas** in the Torah portion. The purpose: to make the Torah portion real, in ways that we can relate to. Every Torah portion contains unique ideas, and when you put all

of those ideas together, you actually come up with a list of Judaism's most important ideas.

> Two *divrei Torah* ("words of Torah," or "sermonettes") for each portion. These *divrei Torah* explain significant aspects of the Torah portion in accessible, reader-friendly language. Each *devar Torah* contains references to **traditional** Jewish sources (those that were written before the modern era), as well as **modern** sources and quotes. We have searched, far and wide, to find sources that are unusual, interesting, and not just the "same old stuff" that many people already know about the Torah portion. Why did we include these minisermons in the volume? Not because we want you to simply copy those sermons and pass them off as your own (that would be cheating), though you are free to quote from them. We included them so that you can see what is possible—how you can try to make meaning for yourself out of the words of Torah.

> **Connections:** This is perhaps the most valuable part. It's a list of questions that you can ask yourself, or that others might help you think about—any of which can lead to the creation of your *devar Torah.*

Note: you don't have to like everything that's in a particular Torah portion. Some aren't that loveable. Some are hard to understand; some are about religious practices that people today might find confusing, and even offensive; some contain ideas that we might find totally outmoded.

But this doesn't have to get in the way. After all, most kids spend a lot of time thinking about stories that contain ideas that modern people would find totally bizarre. Any good medieval fantasy story falls into that category.

And we also believe that, if you spend just a little bit of time with those texts, you can begin to understand what the author was trying to say.

This volume goes one step further. Sometimes, the haftarah comes off as a second thought, and no one really thinks about it. We have tried to solve that problem by including a **summary** of each haftarah, and then a mini-sermon on the haftarah. This will help you learn how these sacred words are relevant to today's world, and even to your own life.

All Bible quotations come from the NJPS translation, which is found in the many different editions of the JPS TANAKH; in the Conservative movement's *Etz Hayim: Torah and Commentary;* in the Reform movement's *Torah: A Modern Commentary;* and in other Bible commentaries and study guides.

How Do I Write a *Devar Torah?*

It really is easier than it looks.

There are many ways of thinking about the *devar Torah.* It is, of course, a short sermon on the meaning of the Torah (and, perhaps, the haftarah) portion. It might even be helpful to think of the *devar Torah* as a "book report" on the portion itself.

The most important thing you can know about this sacred task is: *Learn* the words. *Love* the words. Teach people what it could mean to *live* the words.

Here's a basic outline for a *devar Torah:*

"My Torah portion is (name of portion)_____,
    from the book of _____, chapter

_____.

"In my Torah portion, we learn that_____
    (Summary of portion)

"For me, the most important lesson of this Torah portion is (what is the best thing in the portion? Take the portion as a whole; your *devar Torah* does not have to be only, or specifically, on the verses that you are reading).

"As I learned my Torah portion, I found myself wondering:
> *Raise a question that the Torah portion itself raises.*
> *"Pick a fight"* with the portion. Argue with it.
> *Answer a question* that is listed in the "Connections" section of each Torah portion.
> *Suggest a question to your rabbi* that you would want the rabbi to answer in his or her own *devar Torah* or sermon.

"I have lived the values of the Torah by _____
(here, you can talk about how the Torah portion relates to your
own life. If you have done a mitzvah project, you can talk about
that here).

How To Keep It from Being Boring
(and You from Being Bored)

Some people just don't like giving traditional speeches. From our perspective, that's really okay. Perhaps you can teach Torah in a different way—one that makes sense to you.

> Write an "open letter" to one of the characters in your Torah portion. "Dear Abraham: I hope that your trip to Canaan was not too hard . . ." "Dear Moses: Were you afraid when you got the Ten Commandments on Mount Sinai? I sure would have been . . ."
> Write a news story about what happens. Imagine yourself to be a television or news reporter. "Residents of neighboring cities were horrified yesterday as the wicked cities of Sodom and Gomorrah were burned to the ground. Some say that God was responsible . . ."
> Write an imaginary interview with a character in your Torah portion.
> Tell the story from the point of view of another character, or a minor character, in the story. For instance, tell the story of the Garden of Eden from the point of view of the serpent. Or the story of the Binding of Isaac from the point of view of the ram, which was substituted for Isaac as a sacrifice. Or perhaps the story of the sale of Joseph from the point of view of his coat, which was stripped off him and dipped in a goat's blood.
> Write a poem about your Torah portion.
> Write a song about your Torah portion.
> Write a play about your Torah portion, and have some friends act it out with you.
> Create a piece of artwork about your Torah portion.

The bottom line is: Make this a joyful experience. Yes—it could even be fun.

The Very Last Thing You Need to Know at This Point

The Torah scroll is written without vowels. Why? Don't *sofrim* (Torah scribes) know the vowels?

Of course they do.

So, why do they leave the vowels out?

One reason is that the Torah came into existence at a time when sages were still arguing about the proper vowels, and the proper pronunciation.

But here is another reason: The Torah text, as we have it today, and as it sits in the scroll, is actually *an unfinished work*. Think of it: the words are just sitting there. Because they have no vowels, it is as if they have no voice.

When we read the Torah publicly, we give voice to the ancient words. And when we find meaning in those ancient words, and we talk about those meanings, those words jump to life. They enter our lives. They make our world deeper and better.

Mazal tov to you, and your family. This is your journey toward Jewish maturity. Love it.

THE TORAH

❖ Shemot: Exodus 1:1–6:1

When we last saw Jacob's family, they had settled down in the Goshen region of Egypt. Everyone was happy. Everyone was (finally!) getting along. Generations have now passed since Jacob's son Joseph and his brothers have settled in Egypt. The Israelites have grown numerous, and probably prosperous as well. But the new Egyptian king doesn't know, and could care less, about everything that Joseph had done for Egypt. The Egyptians become afraid of the Israelites, and Pharaoh decides to enslave them. Then he embarks upon an even more evil plan: to kill Israelite children.

All seems lost—until a hero emerges: Moses, born into slavery, adopted by Pharaoh's daughter, a man who figures out that the Israelites are his people, and will have the God-given courage to approach Pharaoh and plead for his people's freedom.

Summary

> Jacob's children and descendants have become comfortable in Egypt. But a new king arises who institutes a program of oppression and enslavement. (1:1–14)

> Two midwives, Shiphrah and Puah, defy Pharaoh's orders to kill Israelite children, and they become the inventors of civil disobedience. (1:15–22)

> A Hebrew boy is born. His parents, fearing for his life, send him floating in a basket down the Nile River. Pharaoh's daughter finds him, adopts him, and gives him the name "Moses." (2:1–10)

> Moses realizes that he is a Hebrew. He fights back against Egyptian oppressors, ultimately fleeing from Egypt to the land of Midian. He marries Zipporah, the daughter of Jethro, a Midianite priest, and they have two sons. (2:11–22)

> Moses encounters God at a bush that burns but is not consumed by fire. God gives him his mission: to lead the Israelites out of Egypt. (3:1–4:23)

The Big Ideas

> **Jewish history has a predictable pattern.** The beginning of Exodus establishes the pattern for much of Jewish history: thriving, success, increased vulnerability, and, ultimately, persecution. This pattern has changed, however, in the United States and other places around the world.

> **Women's roles are crucial in Judaism.** The redemption from Egypt could not have happened without the heroic acts of righteous women: Shiphrah and Puah; Jochebed (Moses's birth mother); Miriam (Moses's sister); and Pharaoh's daughter, who adopted Moses.

> **It's a mitzvah to protest immoral orders.** In fact, that is how people become moral heroes. Here, the lesson of Shiphrah and Puah is crucial. They silently protested the evil plans of Pharaoh, and they saved the lives of the Hebrew children. They were the "inventors" of civil disobedience.

> **To be a Jew means taking care of your own people, and other people as well.** That is the lesson of Moses's early life. He begins by intervening when he sees his own people being persecuted (yet, how does he know that these are his people?), and then he intervenes when shepherds are harassing Jethro's daughters. Jews cannot only think and act on behalf of themselves; they have to think and act on behalf of others as well.

> **The Jews are an eternal people.** God deliberately speaks to Moses out of a bush that burns but is not consumed by fire—which is a symbol of Jewish history. The Jews have often suffered but they have not been consumed by their suffering.

Divrei Torah

THEY SAID, "NO!"

You know how there are "coming attractions" from the next episode at the end of some television shows? That's what the first chapter of Exodus is—the coming attractions for all of Jewish history. Jewish immigrants in Egypt thrive, just as Jews have thrived in many times and places. A new king forgets what Joseph had done for Egypt; in the past, new governments often forgot previous Jewish contributions to their societies. Increasingly, the Egyptians think of the Israelites as a foreign element. The Egyptians begin to question the Israelites' loyalty to Egypt—just as Jews have often been seen as disloyal foreigners in the lands in which they have lived.

Then: persecution, slavery, mass murder. It's all too familiar.

Enter two of the most extraordinary characters of the Hebrew Bible: Shiphrah and Puah, a pair of midwives, whose job it is to help women give birth. Pharaoh commanded them to kill Hebrew infant boys and to let Hebrew girls live. But they refused to do so.

Shiphrah and Puah were the originators of civil disobedience. They are the first people in the Torah to question and defy authority. When a bus driver in Montgomery, Alabama, told Rosa Parks to sit in the back of the bus, where African Americans were then supposed to sit, she refused. It was as if she were channeling Shiphrah and Puah. Perhaps Reverend Martin Luther King Jr. was thinking of them when he said: "An unjust law is a human law that is not rooted in eternal law." King was sitting in jail because he refused to obey an unjust law, and he urged nonviolent civil disobedience against segregation.

An interesting question: Were these midwives Jews or Egyptians? The text says that they were *m'yaldot ivriot* (Hebrew midwives). But according to an alternative understanding of the Hebrew grammar, you can also read that as "midwives *for the Hebrew women.*"

So, were they Hebrew (Israelite) women? Their names are certainly Hebrew. But would Pharaoh really have had Hebrew women kill their own people? It is far more interesting to believe that they were, in fact, Egyptians who saved Jewish lives. Otherwise, how could Pharaoh have told them to kill Jews? The Roman Jewish historian Josephus says that the midwives were certainly Egyptian: "for this office was, by Pharaoh's orders, to be performed by women who, as compatriots of the king, were not likely to transgress his will."

Shiphrah and Puah were good people who saved Jewish lives. It is easier for people to help save their own kin than people they don't know, and much more difficult for people from the "in" group to help people from the "out" group. Think of the "righteous gentiles" who rescued Jews during the Holocaust. If Shiphrah and Puah were, in fact, non-Israelites, it makes their actions even more courageous.

TIME TO GROW UP

Every kid asks this question, usually right around bar and bat mitzvah time: how do I know that I have really grown up?

Let's ask Moses that question.

Moses is a Hebrew, but Pharaoh's daughter found him and raised him as her own child, in Pharaoh's palace. Moses could have had a very cushy life. But, at a certain point, he figures out that he is a Hebrew. How does he figure that out? The Torah doesn't say.

But we do know this: Moses sees an Egyptian torturing a Hebrew slave, and he kills the Egyptian. It would have been nice if Moses didn't have to do that. When the text tells us that Moses "turned this way and that" before killing the Egyptian, maybe he wasn't looking to see whether there were any witnesses around. Maybe he was looking to see whether there were any other people around who could help. But no, Moses was totally alone, and he had to act with courage and with speed.

The next day, Moses sees two Hebrews fighting, and this time he doesn't respond with force. Rather than letting his fists do the talking, he asks a question. Like all good Jewish questions, it starts with "Why?" "Why do you strike your fellow?" (2:13).

At that moment, Moses's childhood ends. As you journey through your teenage years, and as you approach adulthood, you will figure out that a major part of growing up is learning to ask good questions. That has always been the Jewish way: to ask questions whenever possible, and to act decisively when necessary.

The next stop on Moses's journey to maturity is when he flees to Midian, and he sees shepherds harassing Jethro's daughters at the well. Moses sticks up for the women, and drives the harassers away. Moses has no real responsibility for them; they are not his family or his people. But, at that moment, Moses goes beyond the borders of his own family and people and intervenes for the sake of others.

As I have written: "Bonding yourself with your people; responding to their pain; questioning injustice; responding to the pain of those who are outside your people—these are all essential moments on the journey toward adulthood."

We all need role models who can teach us about standing up for ourselves, and for others. For Jews, Shiphrah and Puah are those role models, and so is Moses.

In the words of the sage Hillel: "In a place where there are no men, strive to be a man." Of course, Hillel didn't just mean "men." He meant that it is everyone's job to stand up, be counted, and make a difference. In a situation when no else is willing to stand out and stand up, making a difference can make all the difference!

Connections

> What actions of Moses do you most admire? What actions of Moses do you wish that you will be able to emulate?

> In what way does chapter 1 of Exodus establish a pattern of Jewish history? In what countries has that pattern existed?

> What Jewish women do you admire most?

> From what people do you think that Shiphrah and Puah came—Egyptian or Hebrew? Does it matter? Why or why not?

> Would you have the courage to defy illegal orders or unjust laws? Would you risk your life to save someone you don't know? In the spirit of these two remarkable women, what can you do for other people who need your help?

> What historical figures have behaved like Shiphrah and Puah?

> Have you ever stuck up for someone who was weaker? What was that experience like?

> How will you know when you have become an adult?

THE HAFTARAH

❖ Shemot: Isaiah 27:6–28:13; 29:22–23

One little word—that's all it takes to link this week's haftarah with its Torah portion. The reading in the Torah begins with a report of the Israelites who had come (*ha-ba'im*) into Egypt and become slaves. That occurrence of *ha-ba'im* was not so good. Here in the haftarah the prophet Isaiah also begins with *ha-ba'im*: "in days to come [or, in coming days] Israel shall sprout and blossom." Much better.

In the year 722 BCE, the Assyrian Empire conquered the Northern Kingdom of Israel and scattered its inhabitants, who subsequently came to be known as the "Ten Lost Tribes." Isaiah predicts the day will come when the lost tribes will come home. And not only the tribes whom the Assyrians had exiled, but also those exiles who had somehow wound up in Egypt.

This will be like a new exodus from Egypt—yet another link with the Torah portion, in which God promises Moses that the Israelites will be redeemed from Egypt. Those who are faithful to God will become solidly rooted in the Land of Israel; those who are not will be uprooted.

The Mystery of the Ten Lost Tribes

You probably don't know this, because you have probably been asleep in the middle of the night, when there are television shows with names like "The Bible's Mysteries Revealed." One of the favorite topics is: "Whatever happened to the Ten Lost Tribes of Israel?"

Here's what happened to them: When the Assyrians destroyed the Northern Kingdom of Israel, they carried away the inhabitants and scattered them. And no one knows who and where they are. The Ten Lost Tribes disappeared from history. A legend arose that the tribes went on to live on the other side of the mysterious Sambatyon River (which was said to have stopped flowing in honor of Shabbat). Rumors of other sightings continued throughout history and are rather amazing. One traveler in the 1600s reported that he had found an Indian tribe in South America that could say the *Shema*.

The Jews of Ethiopia have long maintained that they are descended from the ancient tribe of Dan. And there are three groups in India that observe Jewish customs and believe they are descended from the lost tribes: the Bene Ephraim of Telugu in southern India, the Bnei Menashe in northern India, and the Bene Israel. There is also the Lemba, a tribe in Zimbabwe and South Africa; they observe certain Jewish customs, and a DNA study shows that there may be some Jewish linkages.

Some people thought that Native Americans were part of the lost tribes, and that that is why Columbus may have brought along an interpreter who spoke Hebrew. Others believed that the British are descended from the lost tribes, and that the British royal family is directly descended from King David. There is even a legend that the Coronation Stone on which British monarchs were crowned was actually the stone that Jacob slept on when he dreamed of the ladder of angels!

Chances are, no one is ever going to find the Ten Lost Tribes of the Northern Kingdom of Israel. They were probably scattered among other peoples in the ancient Near East. In 1889, Jewish scholar Adolf Neubauer wrote: "Where are the ten tribes? We can only answer—nowhere."

So you might ask: why have people been so fascinated by this subject? Perhaps because to claim that you are a descendant of the people of the Bible is a powerful idea. Jewish teachings, as expressed by the Hebrew Bible, are important to many around the globe, and some have wanted to stake their claim to being part of this remarkable people.

The Talmud teaches: "The Ten [Lost] Tribes will enter the future world, as it is said: 'And in that day, a great ram's horn shall be sounded; and the strayed who are in the land of Assyria and the expelled who are in the land of Egypt shall come and worship the Lord on the holy mount, in Jerusalem.'"

While this has not actually come to pass, think of all the "lost" Jews who have returned to modern Israel. You could say that this miracle has come true.

❖ Notes

❖ Notes

Lightning Source UK Ltd.
Milton Keynes UK
UKHW041028271122
412821UK00016B/202